TOUGH DOGS

GREAT DANES

Julie Fiedler

The Rosen Publishing Group's
PowerKids Press™
New York

For Kibby

Published in 2006 by The Rosen Publishing Group, Inc.
29 East 21st Street, New York, NY 10010

First Edition

Editor: Jennifer Way
Book Design: Elana Davidian

Photo Credits: Cover (left) © Margot Conte/Animals Animals; Cover (right), pp. 15, 19 © Gerard Lacz/Animals Animals; p. 4 © Eunice Pearcy/Animals Animals; p. 7 (top) © Jerry Shulman/SuperStock; p. 7 (bottom) © Don Mason/Corbis; p. 8 © Snark/Art Resource, NY; p. 11 © Hulton-Deutsch Collection/Corbis; p. 12 (top) © Urlike Schanz/Animals Animals; p. 12 (bottom) © Hanna-Barbera, Courtesy Everett Collection; p. 16 © Royalty-Free/Corbis; p. 20 © Bettman/Corbis.

Library of Congress Cataloging-in-Publication Data

Fiedler, Julie.
  Great Danes / Julie Fiedler.— 1st ed.
      p. cm. — (Tough dogs)
  Includes bibliographical references (p.   ) and index.
  ISBN 1-4042-3122-6 (lib. bdg.)
  1. Great Dane—Juvenile literature. I. Title.

  SF429.G7F54 2006
  636.73—dc22

                                    2005001475

Manufactured in the United States of America

Contents

229 4715

The Great Dane is a breed of dog that loves being around people. They can be a welcome addition to a family that is prepared for the special needs of such a large dog. Because of this breed's size, some people are afraid of Great Danes, but they are not naturally mean.

Meet the Great Dane

The Great Dane is a large **breed** of dog that is often called a gentle giant. This is because they are very loving and **devoted**, but very large. Great Danes may look scary, but do not let their big size frighten you away. Their **temperament** is friendly, sweet, and gentle.

Great Danes are brave and strong and were originally used for hunting animals such as wild boar. Because Great Danes were brave hunters and were so large and powerful, people later started training them for use as guard dogs. Today they sometimes work as guard dogs because they are very protective of their owners. These intelligent and active dogs are also used as working dogs and show dogs. However, because Great Danes make such wonderful companions, they are often family pets.

What a Great Dane Looks Like

The easiest way to recognize Great Danes is by their huge size. They range from 30 to 32 inches (76–81 cm) tall at the shoulder and generally weigh 100 to 150 pounds (45–68 kg). Their short, thick coats can be many different colors, including light brown, blue, black, and harlequin, which is white with black patches. They can also have a brindle coat, which is a mix of golden and black stripes. Their almond-shaped eyes are usually dark in color. Their eyes can be light, but that is more rare.

These giant dogs have slender heads with long **muzzles**. Great Danes are born with floppy ears, but their ears can be cropped, or cut, to be pointed. Cropping was originally done to protect their ears from being bitten while they were hunting. Some owners now do not crop their Great Danes' ears. Their tails and legs are long. Their broad chests and strong bodies make Great Danes one of today's most powerful dogs.

Great Danes come in several colors and coat patterns. This Great Dane (above) has a harlequin coat. Inset: This is a brindle-coated Great Dane. Both of these dogs' ears have been cropped so that they stand up. Leaving the ears natural and long has become an increasingly popular choice for owners.

This is an Egyptian painting from around 6000 B.C. The large dogs shown here are believed to be one of the ancestors of many of today's big dogs, including Great Danes.

Ancestors of the Great Dane

The Great Dane's **ancestors** are believed to be large dogs from an **ancient** kingdom in Asia that was called Assyria. Pictures from around 2000 B.C. show these Assyrian dogs hunting and being walked on leashes. These giant dogs look very powerful and look much like today's Great Danes.

Around 500 B.C., the people of Assyria traded goods with other countries. Historians believe that Assyrians also traded these large hunting dogs. Pictures of dogs that look like the Assyrian dogs have been found in art from ancient Rome and Greece from around this time. Soon after that the breed could be found in Europe.

These hunting dogs are believed to be relatives of some of today's biggest breeds, such as the Great Dane and the **mastiff**.

History of the Great Dane

Great Danes were first **bred** in Germany and England in the 1500s, where they were used to hunt boar. Later they were used as guard dogs. It is believed that people at that time wanted a hunting dog that would be large like the mastiff and fast like the Irish wolfhound. They bred these two dogs together to form Great Danes.

Great Danes became popular around the world in the 1800s. In Germany Great Danes were so popular that they became that country's national dog in 1876. In 1857, a man named Francis Butler brought the Great Dane to the United States. Twenty years later owners began to enter Great Danes in dog shows in the United States. Great Danes have always been prized for their strength and appearance. Today they are also prized for their intelligence and good nature.

This 1925 photograph shows Felix of Oakenwood. He was a Great Dane who was the winner of a dog show. The Great Dane did not come from Denmark, as its name suggests. The French called these dogs grand Danois, which means "Great Dane," but it is not known why they were called that.

Above: *This is a blue-coated Great Dane.* Left: *Scooby Doo is a popular cartoon Great Dane. Scooby and his friends have been solving crimes on television and in the movies since 1969.*

The Great Dane Today

Today Great Danes play many different roles. Because they are **obedient**, Great Danes can be trained for different activities, such as tracking, police work, and even dog sports. Great Danes also enter in dog shows that judge dogs based on their appearance and temperament. Most often Great Danes are watchdogs or family pets.

Many people enjoy these large dogs. They are brave and have helped guard homes and save people's lives. Because of their sweet nature, they also make wonderful pets and can be good with children. Some people fear that Great Danes are **aggressive** because they are so large, but the breed is very gentle.

Two of the most-recognized Great Danes are fictional characters. Scooby Doo from the cartoon and movies and Marmaduke from the comic strip of the same name are both Great Danes.

A Tough Breed?

In the 1800s, Great Danes were bred to be aggressive dogs because they were used for hunting and security. Many people were afraid of them, and they were not allowed to enter dog shows for several years. For this reason people today still believe that Great Danes are **fierce**, as their early relatives were.

After Great Danes came to the United States in the 1800s, American breeders decided to improve the Great Dane's temperament. By choosing the gentlest Great Danes and breeding them, breeders were able to get rid of the dogs' aggressiveness. This is known as selective breeding. Today Great Danes are not tough like their ancestors. However, to help make sure that Great Danes continue to be obedient, owners must take good care of them and provide proper care and training.

Because of their size and strength, it is important for Great Danes to be well trained. It is important to begin training when Great Danes are 3 to 6 months old, since it is much easier to train a 25-pound (11 kg) puppy than a 150-pound (68 kg) adult!

Bathing a Great Dane about once a month helps keep the dog's coat clean. Brushing the coat between baths also helps keep the coat smooth and clean.

16

Caring for a Great Dane

No matter which breed of dog you have, it is important to care for it properly. Good care requires providing shelter, healthy food, water, exercise, and lots of love. Great Danes' coats need regular **grooming** to keep their fur smooth and clean. Owners must also take their dogs to the **veterinarian** for regular checkups to check them for health problems.

Great Danes can have certain health problems when they get older. Some Great Danes have weak bones. Great Danes, and other large breeds, can have a condition called bloat. This is a stomach problem that can be deadly. Also like other large breeds, Great Danes do not live as long as do smaller dog breeds.

Great Danes have lots of energy and need lots of exercise. If they do not get enough exercise, they might behave badly. Good training can help curb these bad habits and is an important part of caring for any dog.

Training a Great Dane

It is best for Great Danes to be trained when they are younger than five months old. This is because Great Danes grow quickly, and it is easier to train them while they are still small.

There are five commands every dog should learn. They are *sit*, *stay*, *heel*, *down*, and *come*. Learning these commands helps keep a dog well behaved.

Great Danes also need to be brought into contact with many sights, sounds, and smells when they are young. This is called **socialization**. Socialization helps keep dogs from acting aggressively out of fear.

DOG SAFETY TIPS

- Never approach a dog you do not know.
- When meeting a dog, offer the back of your hand for the dog to sniff.
- Speak softly, not loudly. Move gently, not suddenly.
- Never try to pet a dog through a fence.
- Never bother a dog while it is sleeping, eating, or sick.
- Do not pull at a dog's fur, ears, or tail. Never tease or hit a dog.
- Never approach a dog that is growling or showing its teeth. Back away slowly. Yelling and running can cause the dog to chase you or act aggressively.

Properly socialized dogs will be well behaved around new people and in new surroundings. This Great Dane has been socialized, so it can play with other dogs without acting aggressively out of fear. Socialization and training also help the Great Dane play more carefully so it does not hurt people or smaller dogs by mistake.

This is Major. He was a police dog in Great Britain in the 1960s. In this picture he is posing wearing a hat like those worn by British police officers. Working Great Danes can do many jobs, including search and rescue and working with police.

A Brave Breed

Great Danes have carried out many brave deeds. A Great Dane named Top was a pet in California. One day in 1969, Top's 11-year-old neighbor took him for a walk. As they crossed the street, the girl did not see an oncoming truck, but Top did and he pushed the girl out of harm's way. Top was not so lucky. The truck hit Top and broke his leg. Top was in a cast for seven weeks.

The week after Top had his cast removed, he was playing near a pool while his owner was in the house. Top ran to the door and started barking loudly. The owner ran outside to see what was wrong and saw a neighborhood child drowning in the pool. The owner was able to save the child, thanks to Top. Top won the Ken-L Ration Dog Hero of the Year Award. Having saved two children, he certainly earned it. Top was a true hero.

Many famous people have owned Great Danes, including actors Jim Carrey and Bruce Lee.

What a Dog!

In 2004, around 9,500 Great Danes were listed with the American Kennel Club. Great Danes are ranked as one of the most popular breeds in the United States.

One special example of this breed was a Great Dane named Gracie. Gracie was an **albino** dog who was often sick. Two men named Dan Dye and Mark Beckloff adopted her. As Gracie grew up, she was not able to eat regular dog food. Her owners baked special food and treats for her and even opened a bakery for dogs called Three Dog Bakery. Gracie appeared on TV shows, such as *Late Night with Conan O'Brien*. A book called ***Amazing** Gracie* was written about her. Gracie's loving nature convinced other people to adopt pets even if they have special needs.

Great Danes are a wonderful breed of dog. It is important to value and respect this noble, brave, and intelligent breed.

Glossary

aggressive (uh-GREH-siv) Ready to fight.

albino (al-BY-noh) Lacking color in the skin and eyes.

amazing (uh-MAYZ-ing) Wonderful.

ancestors (AN-ses-terz) Relatives who lived long ago.

ancient (AYN-chent) Very old, from a long time ago.

bred (BRED) Brought a male and a female animal together so they will have babies.

breed (BREED) A group of animals that look alike and have the same relatives.

devoted (dih-VOHT-ed) Faithful.

fierce (FEERS) Strong and ready to fight.

grooming (GROOM-ing) Cleaning the body and making it appear neat.

mastiff (MAS-tif) A breed of very large dog.

muzzles (MUH-zuhlz) The parts of animals' heads that come forward and include the nose.

obedient (oh-BEE-dee-ent) Willing to do what you are told to do.

socialization (soh-shuh-lih-ZAY-shun) Learning to be friendly.

temperament (TEM-pur-ment) Character, nature.

veterinarian (veh-tuh-ruh-NER-ee-un) A doctor who treats animals.

Index

A
American Kennel Club, 22
ancestors, 9, 14

B
bloat, 17
Butler, Francis, 10

C
coat(s), 6, 17

E
ears, 6
eyes, 6

G
Gracie, 22

grooming, 17
guard dogs, 5, 10

H
hunting, 5–6, 9–10, 14

I
Irish wolfhound, 10

M
mastiff, 9–10
muzzles, 6

P
pets, 5, 13

S
show dogs, 5,
socialization, 18

T
tail(s), 6
Three Dog Bakery, 22
Top, 21
training, 14, 17–18

V
veterinarian, 17

W
working dogs, 5

Web Sites

Due to the changing nature of Internet links, PowerKids Press has developed an online list of Web sites related to the subject of this book. This site is updated regularly. Please use this link to access the list:
www.powerkidslinks.com/tdog/greatdane/

24